# Kanban

## Step-by-Step Guide to Kanban

### (Core Practices, Kanban Systems, Full Value Chain, Forecasting with Kanban)

*Jason Bennett & Jennifer Bowen*

# Table of Contents

# Introduction

I want to thank you for choosing this book, 'Kanban'

Kanban is a tool that is used by most organizations to visualize and limit work-in-progress or bottlenecks in any project in the organization. Kanban loosely translates to signal card or signboard in Japanese. This tool was developed in the early 1940s by Taiichi Ohno to improve the performance of Toyota.

Toyota sent a card to the supplier to let them know that they needed more quantities of a certain part and the same card was stuck to the part when it was sent to Toyota. When the parts were used, the same card was sent to the manufacturers and suppliers to let them know that the part was needed again.

This helped the company assemble the products on time and send them to the customers.

The same process can be applied to different organizations in different industries.

Kanban boards and Kanban software allow a manager or an entire team understand how a task is progressing. Through these tools, they can understand impediments and identify ways to remove those impediments. Over the course of the book, you will gather information on what Kanban is and how it can be used to improve quality of work.

There are different principles and practices that any organization must adhere to when implementing Kanban systems. It is important that a team manager and members of the team understand these practices and function well. There are numerous benefits of using the Kanban tool at work since it increases productivity and improves quality.

This book will help you understand how Kanban systems can be used in different departments in the company and how the principles can be applied to different industries. Kanban can also be used to predict the outcomes of certain processes using certain statistical tools like graphs and simulations. This aspect is touched upon in the last chapter of the book.

An advantage of Kanban is that it can be used to improve visibility in an organization since every process is viewed as an image and each task within that process is identified and completed.

Kanban can also be used to improve an individual's work ethic.

Thank you for purchasing the book. I hope you have gathered all the information you were looking for.

# Chapter One: An Introduction to Kanban

Kanban is a system that was developed to manage work while it is in process/progress. Through the boards available in the management system, one can visualize the process or the workflow and the actual work that is moving through the process.

The goal of the system is to identify potential impediments or bottlenecks in the process and fix them to improve workflow.

## A Brief History

Taiichi Ohno, the Japanese Industrial Businessman and Engineer for Toyota automotive developed Kanban in the early 1940s. The system was created to help different teams plan their work and address any issues that arose during the workflow.

The software aimed to manage work at every stage of the process.

Kanban was developed since the Toyota business in Japan was not functioning as well when compared to the rivals in America. With the use of Kanban, Toyota achieved control systems that helped to increase their productivity. It also helped to reduce the wastage of any raw material that was used.

A Kanban system controls the value chain right from a supplier of raw material to the customer. This helps to avoid any disruption in supply and also reduces any surplus of goods at different stages of the process.

This software requires constant monitoring, and particular attention must be given to view potential bottlenecks and avoid them from the start to improve the process. Every company aims to achieve high output with low delivery times. Over the years, Kanban has been used in multiple systems to improve efficiency.

## What is the Kanban Method?

The Kanban method was introduced in the manufacturing industry by Taiichi Ohno but was applied in the IT industry, knowledge work and software development in the year 2004 by David Anderson. David used the work by Eli Goldratt, Peter Drucker, Edward Demmings, Taiichi Ohno and others to define the method using concepts like queuing theory, pull systems and flow.

## Kanban Change Management Principles

The Kanban method follows a list of practices and principles that help to improve and manage the workflow. The method is non-disruptive and evolutionary. It helps to improve the processes that are worked on in an organization.

Your organization will successfully be able to implement the principles and practices of Kanban to maximize the benefits of every business process by improving the workflow, reducing delivery time and increasing customer satisfaction.

The foundational principles and practices of the method have been listed below.

# Foundational Principles

## *Always start with what you are doing now*

The Kanban method does not require you to make any changes to your process right away. Instead, use the method on the current workflow and make changes to the flow when needed and over a period. You have to ensure that your team is on board with any changes you make to the process.

## *Pursue evolutionary and incremental change*

The Kanban system encourages every team and its members to make small changes instead of making significant changes that can lead to resistance from the members of the team and the organization.

## *Respect Current Roles, Responsibilities and Designations*

Unlike most methods, Kanban does not impose any changes to the structure of the organization. You do not have to make any changes to the existing functions and roles that may not be performing too well. Through Kanban, the team will identify the changes and implement them when needed. The first three principles help an organization overcome the fear of change.

## *Encourage Acts of Leadership*

Since the Kanban system encourages continuous improvement at every level of the organization, leadership acts do not have only to be performed by senior managers. People at every level are allowed to show leadership and identify ways to change the process. They are encouraged to identify ways to improve how products and services are delivered.

# Core Practices

## Visualize the workflow

When you adopt and use the Kanban method, you must visualize the workflow. You must visualize the steps either on a physical board or a Kanban board to identify the steps being taken to deliver work or any other service. A Kanban board can either be simple or complex depending on the different types of work items that teams will need to work on and deliver.

Once the processes have been visualized, you must visualize the current work that is being done by the team. This can be done using cards with different colors or notes to identify the different classes of work being performed by the team. You can include different columns and colors to define the processes and work that is being done by every member of the team and the team on the whole. These boards can always be redesigned to improve a process.

## Limit or Reduce Work-in-Progress

It is important to limit work-in-progress to implement the Kanban system. This will encourage your team to complete work that is ongoing before taking up any new project. It means that the team can only take up a new process when work that is in progress is marked complete. This increases the team's capacity to bring in more work.

It may not be easy to identify the limit of work-in-progress. You may begin with no WIP limits, and Don Reinertsen had suggested that a team should start with no WIP limits and then observe how the team performs when you begin to use Kanban. When you have sufficient data, you can define your WIP limits at every stage of the workflow.

Most teams start with a WIP limit that is either 1 or 1.5 times the number of people in the team working on a specific task.

It is beneficial to the team to limit WIP and put WIP limits since the team members will finish their tasks before they move onto new tasks. This also communicates to the stakeholders and customers that there is a limited capacity of work that can be performed by the team. Therefore, careful planning must be involved when any new task or request is made to the team.

## Manage Flow

It is essential to manage and improve workflow when you have implemented and mastered the first two activities. A Kanban system helps the team manage workflow by highlighting different stages of the workflow and the status of work that needs to be completed at each stage. The WIP limits are set depending on the how the workflow has been defined. Any team will notice that the work is being completed on time within the WIP limits or the work is being piled up since there is one task that is held up. This affects the speed at which the team can deliver work.

Kanban helps a team analyze the system and also make adjustments to the system to improve workflow. It also allows teams to understand how they can reduce the time taken to complete one task. It is essential to look at the intermediate wait stages to observe work, resolve and eliminate bottlenecks in the workflow. A team should analyze how long they are in the intermediate wait stages and identify ways to reduce the time spent in those stages. This is a crucial step to consider when the team is looking to reduce the cycle time.

As workflow improves, a team's delivery becomes predictable and smoother. When it becomes predictable, it becomes more comfortable for the team to realize the commitments made to the customers and complete the work within the time frame. It is essential for the team to identify a way to forecast completion times, as it helps to improve the team's functionality.

## *Make Policies Explicit*

As part of visualizing a process, it makes sense for a team to explicitly define and visualize policies that explain how the work provided is done. A team manager or project manager must create a policy that defines how work must be completed in the system. The policies can be prepared at a board level, for each column or at a swim lane level. These policies could include checklists that must be ticked off at every step of the process. These lists should be made for every task that is performed by the team to help team members manage the workflow. For example, the definition of when a task is deemed complete or the description of when tasks can be pulled or pushed must be included in the policies.

## *Feedback Loops*

Feedback loops are an integral part of every sound system, and the Kanban method encourages every team to implement a variety of constructive feedback loops. Every team must look at different stages in the workflow on the Kanban board, reports and metrics that can be used to improve on any processes.

The mantra "Fail fast and fail often," may not always work for different teams and is often not understood by most teams. However, if a team receives feedback at an early stage in the process, the team or project manager will be able to identify a way to deliver the work on time with fewer errors. A feedback loop is crucial to ensure that.

## *Improve and evolve collaboratively and experimentally*

The Kanban method is an improvement process that allows teams to make small changes to the process before making huge improvements. This ensures that teams can handle the changes quickly. This system allows the use of statistical methods where the team builds a hypothesis and tests that hypothesis to understand the outcome.

The critical task for any team is to evaluate and improve a process whenever necessary constantly. The impact of the changes made can be measured and observed using different signals on the Kanban board. These signals help the team evaluate whether the change made to the process is indeed helping the process and can decide whether or not to keep it.

A Kanban system helps the team collect important information about the performance of every member of the team and the team as a whole. This data will help the team generate metrics that can be used to evaluate the performance and tweak the system if needed.

## Is Kanban dead?

There are many people who have not heard of Kanban and there are more people who will tell you that Kanban is now obsolete. However, that is far from the truth. Kanban is a pull system, which unlike push systems, is good. Kanban systems make it easy to track and control work done by different departments in an organization.

There are new methods being developed to make it easy for management to track the work that is being done by teams in an organization. It is true that companies, which are lean, are moving away from Kanban and using newer methods and technologies to maintain workflow. It is also true that most methods being developed use the principles and practices of Kanban.

So, is Kanban dead? No, it is not. There are many changes taking place in the world of lean delivery that improve the productivity of an organization and Kanban is one tool that is changing the world of lean delivery.

# Chapter Two: How does Kanban work

Kanban is a change management system that is both evolutionary and non-disruptive, which means that existing processes are improved by making small changes.

The risk to the overall system is reduced when the team makes small changes instead of large ones. This approach leads to no or low resistance from the team, stakeholders and customers involved.

As mentioned earlier, the team must visualize the processes and the workflow. This can be done using the Kanban board that consists of a simple whiteboard and some sticky notes of different colors. Each note on the board is used to represent a different task.

Three columns are included in a classic Kanban board.

- "To Do": The tasks that are not yet started and are possibly delayed
- "Doing": The tasks that are being worked on by the team
- "Done": The tasks that have been completed

This visualization leads to transparency since the distribution of work is known and the bottlenecks for any task are identified at the start. Kanban boards can show some elaborate workflows depending on how complex the workflow is and which parts of the workflow need to be visualized. This would help the team remove any bottlenecks in complex processes too.

## Concept of Flow

The core of the Kanban system is the concept of flow, which means that the cards used to represent processes must flow through the workflow, as evenly and smoothly possible without any blocks or waiting times.

Any risk that can hinder the flow of work should be examined critically, and the Kanban system has many techniques, models and metrics that can be used. This system helps a team achieve kaizen or a state of constant improvement.

The concept of flow is critical to a process, and if a team views the flow and works on improving it, the speed of delivery can be improved rapidly. This process will also help the team reduce cycle time and improve quality of work by getting faster and more constructive feedback from stakeholders or customers.

## Kanban WIP Limits

Most teams and members are prone to multi-task since they are encouraged to complete as many tasks as possible within a given timeframe. The Kanban system helps to reduce multi-tasking and focuses on the mantra "Stop starting and start finishing."

As mentioned earlier, the team must identify WIP limits at every stage on the Kanban board and encourage members of the team to finish their ongoing tasks before they move onto new tasks.

# Chapter Three: Types of Kanban Systems

Many organizations have started to use Kanban systems to improve their productivity. There are different types of cards that can be used in a Kanban system since Kanban; unlike 6-Sigma is not a fixed methodology.

It is for this reason that it can be used for different purposes. The different types of Kanban systems are listed out in the chapter. This is not an exhaustive list of the Kanban system can mean different things to various organizations.

## Production Kanban

This system is made of an exhaustive list of tasks that must be completed to ensure that a product is delivered on time. This system brings in information on different material and parts that are required along with the information from Withdrawal systems.

This system allows the team to start with the production of the product and also explain the services or products that must be produced.

## Withdrawal Kanban

This system is also known as a conveyance or move cards Kanban. If any component needs to be transferred from the production Kanban to another type, this system is used for signaling.

The cards are connected to different tasks that must be taken to a workplace when they should be completed. Once the tasks are complete, the cards are returned.

## Emergency Kanban

This type of system is used to replace any defective parts or to signal to the entire team that the quantity of a product or service required to be manufactured has either increased or decreased in number.

Organizations often use emergency Kanban systems when a particular part of a system has stopped functioning the way it is supposed to or when there are any changes made to the process.

## Through Kanban

Through Kanban systems comprise both production and withdrawal Kanban systems. These systems are used in situations where both the workstations associated with the two Kanban systems are adjacent to each other. This system speeds the process of production.

For example, if an organization has the area of production and area of storage next to each other, the system will pull parts from the two systems and operate on those parts across the production queue.

## Express Kanban

This system is one that comes into picture when there is a shortage of parts within the system. These systems send signals to the teams to increase the number of parts that are required to complete the process in hand.

This system aims to ensure that the manufacturing process or production process is not slowed down. These systems are often called signal Kanban systems since they are used to trigger any shortage or purchase.

## Supplier Kanban

A supplier is an organization or individual from whom another organization sources material to make its products. This system moves directly towards the supplier and is often entered as a representation of the manufacturer.

Regardless of the type of Kanban system used, it is important to note that a Kanban system is a way to increase productivity and quality of the products and services provided by an organization.

# Chapter Four: Benefits of Kanban

The concept of managing the development of a product is not one that is new. The core philosophy of Kanban has been known widely since its development in the early 1940s.

The principles of product development management and create knowledge work for both Taiichi Ohno's Toyota Production System (TPS) and Lean Manufacturing originate from Kanban.

If a company chose to manage work instead of managing people, it helps to create a balanced, creative, humane and synergetic environment for individuals to unleash their ultimate potential. This strategy is a simple way to make a change in the organization.

This strategy is non-intrusive and has been embraced by many new organizations because it starts with managing the work that is done within the organization.

Let us take a look at how Kanban can help your organization.

## Business Values come first

David Anderson who is considered one of the pioneers of the Kanban method has stated Kanban is not only a method or a system that helps to manage the flow of projects but also a decision management framework that is extremely powerful.

This system has been designed in a way that allows an organization to make decisions that are specific to some economic goals. Since organizations function in competitive environments, they must prioritize, implement and execute tasks as quickly as they can. They must also strive to submit work that is error-free to keep themselves one step ahead of any competitors.

Don Reinertsen has said that a company should always quantify the cost of delaying a product. Alternatively, the organization could also try to assess what the cost of implementing one feature over the other could be since the feature being implemented could be the one that sets the organization apart from others in the same industry. The organization must also calculate the delay in using one feature over another.

## Improves Visibility

A lot of work that is done in an organization is often under the parapet, and it is essential to make that work visible to the leads of the organization and its customers. This is a core attribute of Kanban. Kanban boards can be used as radiators of information to view the progress of a process and any impediments or bottlenecks in the process at a glance.

This information is available not only to the members of the organization but also to any stakeholders, observers and customers. This helps to promote boundary-less information across the organization. The limits in the software help one understand the work that is being viewed and how it is being prioritized.

## Reduces Context-Switching

The number of work items that are being taken care of by employees is numbered in the Kanban system, which is reduced by WIP limits. This focused system helps the employees deliver work items that are both high-priority and high-value which increases the value of your business. Kanban prevents teams from overburdening their members using personal WIP limits.

Any member can only start another task when that member completes the task that they have committed to deliver. This list of Kanban works on the following principle – 'Stop starting, start finishing.' This system has helped many teams focus and successfully deliver downstream activities.

## Improves Collaboration

In most organizations, departments are isolated from one another. There are times when there are battles that exist between software delivery teams and product management. Through Kanban, the teams become integrated into the development value system.

Kanban is a pull-based system that encourages synergies and also breaks the walls down between different departments and specializations, which result in cross-departmental collaboration. The transition of work items on the Kanban boards offers teams the opportunity to share knowledge, collaborate and communicate with one another.

## Reduces Wasteful Activities

Many project managers focus on timelines instead of process queues since the former is embedded deeply in their psyche. They use Gantt charts and other documents to help them assess the timelines for every member of the team.

What most project managers fail to understand is that they must embrace uncertainty and not only granular planning. Most project managers make an effort to design activities that increase the timeline and project risk thereby increasing the process queues.

The Kanban board reinforces some WIP limits that make the system a pull-based system, which allows an organization or team to maintain a reliable number of high-quality ideas that can be delivered within the right timeline. This also helps to eliminate any work that is considered wasteful thereby reducing the number of queues needed to be developed.

Some upstream activities like workshops, requirements gathering and business cases take place on demand and when they are needed. This means that the project manager will need to make timely decisions. Kanban allows the project manager to coordinate multiple activities relevant to validated and prioritized ideas across the board.

## Introduces True Sustainability

Kanban processes help multiple teams manage work at a humane, sustainable and smooth pace. This reduces stress, frustration and lack of commitment thereby increasing employee turnover. WIP limits help to control the pace of a process dynamically thereby fostering creativity.

The teams will never commit to a process initially and break that promise down the road. Teams will be allowed to address and innovate issues in different ways to create solutions that have fewer quality issues.

## Improves Quality

For most professionals, initial quality is an integral part of the successful delivery. Defects can always impact the team's throughput and also help the team tackle any quality issues right from the start, which helps to boost productivity. There are many activities, like collaborative analysis and user documentation that contribute to high-quality software.

The policies in Kanban software strengthen professional standards that are agreed across different boards including project managers, software items, product managers, business stakeholders and customers. The software explicitly defines these policies at every stage of the process.


## Improves Morale

The Kanban software allows many traditional and agile teams to move from pressure and command and control strategies. Every member of the team must build their schedule around the workflow that is organized by the system and not by their managers.

Every member of the team is required to deliver work at a rapid, sustainable and steady pace, which helps to create beneficial stress called eustress thereby allowing members to visualize the fruit of their labor. Since Kanban manages the work of every member of a team, the members are less likely to be stressed, and they always get on with their work and unfold their talents and creativity.

## Instills Kaizen Culture

The Kaizen board provides the managers and team members with queues that are controlled and require shorter buffers. A pull-based system helps to expose any bottlenecks, process inefficiencies, impediments, issues with delivery, miscommunication, agency issues, synergies and lack of clarity.

These queues draw attention to issues and help teams and members identify ways to resolve the issues before development stalls. Through these queues, Kanban introduces Kaizen, which is a concept where a team learns to continuously improve on how it deals with issues observed across the board.

## Introduces Predictability

Kanban was thought to be an information radiator in the past. Through the queues and lists found on the board, Kanban helps a manager predict most issues based on actual or historical data. This reduces the risk of any guesstimate made by a project manager. When improvements are introduced based on actual data, the lead and delivery times improve over time.

There are many benefits to using a Kanban system. An organization will be able to save money and also increase efficiency through the Kanban system. However, there are a few things to keep in mind before setting up the system. The team will need to monitor the amount of work and the different processes that must be completed to deliver on time.

This is a process that takes time, and there is a possibility that the team may account for some processes that are not necessarily important.

It is also essential to remember that there could be a delay in production when trying to understand how Kanban systems work.

To ensure that the system works best for the team it is important to understand the strengths and weaknesses of every member in the team and also assess the time taken by each member to complete a specific task.

A manager must use that information to build a system and divide the processes between the members of the team.

# Chapter Five: Project Management and Kanban

Project management is a concept that can be defined as running an enterprise or following a to-do list to the tee. The idea of project management remains the same regardless of the activities that it comprises. It is important to remember that project management is the only scale that changes within a company.

Most organizations that have used Kanban as a tool for project management will associate project management with visual management.

Nobody in the organization, including the project manager, will have an idea of what is going on in a process if he or she does not have a visual representation of the process available.

Therefore, project management is a way of organizing the steps that need to be fulfilled before the goal of the project is reached.

## How does Kanban help

- With Kanban, work can be assigned and shared between team members. Each of the members is expected to manage their workload based on their priorities and preferences.

- Every member's assignments can be looked at easily and a sketch can be made to understand the problems that the member may face while working on the process.

- If there is a visual record of the processes, it becomes easier to understand if new employees are needed to share the workload.

It also becomes easier to understand if a member needs to be guided.

- Individual and team efficiencies can be identified and measured using the metrics on the Kanban board. It is best to use digital systems since they do the calculations for you reducing the amount of work that would need to be put in.
- Every member of the team gains insights into what process the organization follows and also makes the role of every member easy to understand.

## Common Mistakes made by Project Managers

Project managers often make the mistake of micro-managing people. They take the feeling of empowerment and control from their employees leading to a lack of responsibility. People may also feel that they are not required to work on the processes to achieve the final goal.

Every team should ensure that it is self-organized. The members of the team should plan their work based on their final goal. They should not look at a step-by-step path. If a project manager micro-manages his team, he is wasting his time and his team's time.

## What do you gain by using online project management tools

If a project manager uses online tools, he will be able to identify which member is busy or free and also assess the status of every process or task. These tools will save time since they provide the manager with an idea on how the work is shared, reviewed or commented.

It is best to use online tools like Kanban, since the manager will cut down on the time spent on meetings and communication. There are many companies who turn to online project management since they work in large teams that are distributed across different locations.

## Why is Kanban so effective?

The simplicity of the tool is what makes it so effective. Teams and managers can list any tasks in the backlog on the to-do section of the board and choose tasks that need to be focused on right now. They will not have to worry about missing out on some tasks because of the workload.

There is also a sense of satisfaction and achievement when a card is moved from the to-do list to the done list on the board. This is a simple way to visualize the tasks that are complete and the tasks that are still in progress.

## What makes Kanban versatile

Kanban tools can be used in multiple departments and in different ways since it is a simple tool. There are very few processes where Kanban won't be applicable. Most organizations work with processes that can be envisioned, making a hectic day easier and seem more organized.

The manager and the members of the team can plan their work and also understand if everything is under control using the Kanban board. If the manager is stressed, all he or she needs to do is look at the board and calm down.

# How does Visual Thinking help in planning?

The phrase "A picture is worth a thousand words," is why it is important to visualize the workflow. It is effective to see the tasks that are to be completed in a day listed out on the board than to think about the tasks that will need to be completed and forgetting most of them in the process.

It is believed that most people think visually even if they are not intending to. Visual thinking helps to bring order and to build a structure to constantly interrupted and disorganized thought processes.

# Is there a move towards visual project management in general?

This is true since most businesses, regardless of the size, appreciate the value that visual management and planning bring to the organization. This is proven when one looks at smaller teams.

When smaller teams within an organization begin to perform effectively, the organization will look for more teams to use visual project management. As the knowledge of Kanban spreads through the market, there are more people who wish to incorporate the tool in their business.

If any team is looking to increase productivity, take a look at the following points below:

- Avoid multitasking since it is more of a hindrance. There are some occasions where you will need to multitask since it makes sense to do so.

- Always take breaks since you will feel better and will be able to work more effectively.

- Always finish the most difficult tasks first. It is best to have a day that gets easier by the hour.

- Switch your phone off or switch it to silent when you are working.
- Do not call for too many meetings.

- Prioritize the tasks regularly and make the order of tasks match the needs of the business.

# Chapter Six: Use of Kanban Systems

Kanban is a simple software, which is not just about working with a whiteboard and listing out the tasks for a team using different cards. The first two chapters should have helped you understand that Kanban systems are more than that. An organization will benefit from using Kanban systems if they adhere to the principles and practices of the system.

The current trends show that Kanban is being used in different industries and areas and is gaining immense popularity. Small agencies, start-ups and even traditional organizations have begun to use Kanban systems.

## Kanban in Software and IT

Kanban is not project management or software development tool, and this has been made evident right from the start. Kanban does not talk about how software must be built or provide a list of methods to use to manage a project. It does not talk about how a process should be planned or how software should be implemented.

Therefore, Kanban, unlike Scrum, is a system that helps an organization and teams within that organization improve their work. Microsoft used Kanban in 2004 for its software development operations, and since then it has been used in different software teams across the organization.

The beauty of the system is that it can be applied to multiple methodologies and processes. If an organization is already using agile methods like XP, Scrum and others or traditional methods like iterative or waterfall, Kanban can be applied to those methods to improve processes, improve quality of work and reduce cycle time.

This will help an organization continue to deliver products and services of excellent quality.

## Kanban in Software or Product Development

Many tech product development and application software development teams have used Kanban to implement Agile and Lean principles. The Kanban method gives the teams a great set of practices and principles that will help them visualize their work and deliver products and services at high speed.

These teams will also be able to get constant feedback from customers to help them improve their processes. The teams are also able to market their products to their customers with greater speed.

The Kanban system has undergone an evolution over the last five years in many industries, especially the IT industry. Kanban is considered to be one of the best methods that can be used by teams to manage and improve the services in a gradual manner.

The Kanban method also provides teams with essential techniques and principles that improve Service Level Agreements (SLA), minimize the risk during the process, reduce the cost of delay and deliver products at the right time.

Kanban helps delivery teams and customers collaborate effectively using concepts like Class of Services, 2-phase commit and deferred commitment to ensure that the right processes are worked on at the right times.

Businesses have begun to use Kanban after the advent of Portfolio Kanban. Enterprise Services Planning and Upstream Kanban are used to improve market performance and achieve great agility.

## Kanban and Enterprise Agility

The Kanban method helps an organization improve the delivery of products and services gradually. This is done by removing any bottlenecks or impediments in the system thereby improving the workflow and reducing the time taken to complete a task. This system helps teams deliver continuously and obtain feedback from the customers within a short time span. This feedback allows the team to improve the product or service and helps the team become responsive.

The Kanban system enables the principles of any Agile Manifesto and helps teams deliver products and services that are needed by customers. The Kanban system works with agile methodologies and techniques to improve processes for better performance of the organization.

Kanban is a natural fit for most non-IT business processes since its roots lie in manufacturing. If an organization wants to become lean and agile and deliver products of high quality, it must make use of the Kanban system.

Large and medium organizations have been using 6-Sigma and Lean initiatives to improve their production workflow for several years. However, Kanban systems enable every business, regardless of size or type, to improve every business function like Marketing, HR, Procurement, Sales, etc.

Kanban is being applied in multiple project management contexts including engineering and construction projects. Multiple organizations like recruitment organizations, staffing companies, insurance companies, advertising agencies and many other companies are using Kanban systems to eliminate waste and streamline their processes thereby improving quality and throughput.

# Chapter Seven: How to use Kanban to improve the full value chain

Kanban systems are perfect for organizations, teams and teams within teams since it is a collaborative method. It is for this reason that the boards can work for any department in business and the overall business.

Through Kanban, every department involved in the production of goods and services can identify ways to optimize the process. This chapter provides details on how every department in an organization can use Kanban to improve its working.

## Human Resources and Onboarding

The internal processes, especially HR processes benefit from the use of Kanban boards since they can organize every task at hand. An example of such a process could be the hiring process. When a company advertises job openings, many things start to happen.

- There will be many applicants trying to get in touch with the HR department about the opening and the job description.

- The HR department must gather all the applications and resumes that are being sent to the office.

- If the applicant's resume and application fit the necessary criteria, the HR will need to call the applicant and speak to the concerned people to schedule interviews and go through the different steps that come with any hiring process.

This can be overwhelming for the HR department since there are many people to keep track of and the HR department must know what stage each of the applicants is in. A Kanban board can help to streamline the process and ensure that the HR is aware of the position of every applicant in the process.

There are times when a single board cannot handle the number of applicants. In such instances, Kanban project management software can be used. The software will not only keep track of the board and the cards on the board, but it will also keep track of individual applicants.

There are many internal processes that the HR must deal with, such as onboarding. Since these processes have workflows, they can be dealt with quickly using a Kanban board.

For instance, a visual aid can be made to track any new acquisition and see if they have been trained. Kanban boards work well with the short-term projects that the HR and Learning and Development Teams must work on throughout the year.

## Purchasing

Businesses that rely on incoming shipments can use Kanban cards and boards to keep track of the products that are coming and going out. They can also keep track of when the products are coming in. A Kanban board contains cards that allow every individual in the department to know the status of individual shipments.

A Kanban board offers the department members a quick overview of what is happening with the shipment, which reduces the need to check the files every day to know the progress.

This increases productivity and also allows every individual in the team to know when they can expect the delivery of the product. For shipments that have already reached the premises, the board can identify where the products are being unloaded and how they are going to be distributed.

## Development Department

Any business with a product development department will benefit from the use of Kanban systems because of its collaborative nature. A Kanban system allows for a project to be completed quickly and efficiently. Regardless of whether it is a project, web development or software team, a Kanban board can help facilitate the processes since the team will be able to visualize how the process will progress right from the beginning to the end.

The system can be used for multiple reasons, but at the heart of the Kanban system, it is a project management tool. It is essential to remember that Kanban was started in Toyota to facilitate the manufacturing process. The development, production, manufacturing, assembly and supply departments of the company used this system.

## Sales

As a tracking and visualization tool, Kanban boards help the sales department keep track of the progress made. It is essential for the department to track every aspect of the sale, right from the lead to the end of the deal.

Apart from this, the board can help the department keep track of any post-sale activity including feedback and issues.

Since all the information is available as an image, it becomes more comfortable for the department to improve the process for future sales. This will help businesses work on the sales methods and also help the team understand what works for their department and how they can capitalize on that.

The additional benefit of automation can be obtained by using the Kanban software. For instance, if the leads mentioned on the board never follow up with the department for more information, some triggers can be used to send emails to the leads to keep them involved with the process and move those leads to the next column.

A Kanban board helps members on the sales team to identify the leads that have moved to the next stage of the process. These leads can be color-coded depending on their movement across the board. This gives the team more information about how leads can be converted into potential customers.

## Marketing

A Kanban board can do a lot for a marketing department and for marketing in general. Every marketing strategy comprises many methods and it does get difficult to keep track of the different methods. There are different teams within the marketing department that often butt heads because they are not on the same page. For instance, the marketing department may need to juggle:

- SEO and content marketing
- Social media marketing
- Video Marketing
- Email Marketing
- Print Advertisements
- Connect with potential agencies
- Connect with media or channels

These are some important things that the marketing department must do and it is important that they work together. The Kanban board helps to organize the different efforts that the marketing team must make into a more cohesive list of tasks. This list helps the department stay on track. The department can use a simple board to show the following:

- What tasks are in the backlog or inventory list
- What tasks are running currently
- How soon can those tasks be completed?
- What are the next set of tasks

If the department wants to use a complex board and look at more metrics, it can add more columns to help the department understand the following:

- What is working for the department
- What is not working for the department
- What tasks are falling behind
- What aspects need to be tweaked

The managers can identify the different areas where they would need to put in more focus if they are able to visualize the work that needs to be completed.

## Customer Support

Kanban systems and boards can help the customer support team deal with customer queries or complaints quickly. The team must deal with customers and respond to them as quickly as they can and assist them. Customers may want to send in queries, feedback or complaints at any given time.

If the department uses Kanban systems, any request via email or phone can be turned into a card and that card can be placed at the top of the board.

When the team sees the card, the card must be moved to the next stage immediately. This will ensure that things keep moving along and everybody in the team is aware of how a request from the customer is being handled.

## Helpdesk and IT

Support tickets often overwhelm and flood any help desk. A Kanban board can organize those tickets in order of priority and move them along the board. If a Kanban software is used, the tickets can be ordered based on the priority using color codes. Individuals in the team who are adept at handling such requests can pick the cards.

This process also allows the help desk to identify more significant issues and see what can be done to curb such issues. If there are many people with the same problem, the department can identify what can be done better to improve performance and reduce errors. The Kanban system can also be used to identify a problem.

## Operations

Departments in business represent individual parts of the whole system that must work together to achieve a common goal. The operations team holds the different departments together and is accountable for the functioning of every department.

Since Kanban boards allow every department to see how they are progressing with their work, it can also help them and operations ensure that they are on track with the remaining departments.

Kanban boards are a great way to connect the flow of information or work between different departments and can be used to identify how the work of one department affects another.

# Chapter Eight: How can Kanban be used in back offices

It is important to remember that kaizen is not a tool for Kanban; it is, in fact, the other way around. Kanban is a system or device that can be used by individuals, teams and organizations to think more about their work and how they can work effectively to complete the tasks at hand.

A Kanban system aims to reform a manager's mind. So, how can Kanban be used in a back office?

Think of the first task that you are asked to do in every self-organization book. Every evening or night, sit down and list the tasks that you must finish the following day.

When you reach your office, pull your list out and start with the first task. Ensure that you do not jump to the second or third task without completing the first. Only move to the second task after you have completed your first task. Once your tasks are complete, go about the day as it comes.

This is a powerful tool since our minds are always cluttered with different tasks and all sorts of work that we must do. There are times that we forget to complete tasks that are extremely important because we have too much going on in our head.

If we do not list down tasks based on priority, we will begin to procrastinate and will take on other tasks before the ones we need to compete now.

Often people start working on the first task they can think of when they have too much work to do. If they hit an obstacle, they let go of that task and move onto the next.

The same process goes on until the person has started every task on his or her list but has not completed any of the tasks. He or she will come to realize that half the morning has gone by and not one task has been completed. Let us take a look at the following example.

Bob reached work at 9 AM and has been working on four tasks at the same time without completing any task. It is nearing 5 PM, and he wants to go home, but he has no work to show for the day. A new task has just come in, and he wants to take it up but has absolutely no time since he still has his four tasks left to complete.

He looks at Alice and asks her if she can complete that task within the stipulated time. This creates a backlog or an inventory of future work on Alice's desk since she has her set of tasks to complete.

The Kanban system keeps all new tasks on a central board and only assigns it to a team member if the team has completed all tasks. This type of work has the following advantages:

- Every individual in a team takes on one task and completes it fully. If the tasks do not take up too much time, they can take up two or three tasks and complete them within the stipulated time. This way, they can focus on the tasks at hand. If the inventory or backlog list is smaller every individual will have fewer obstacles to deal with.

- When a team receives the next task, the members will need to think about the following
  - Is this task of high priority?
  - Why does this task need to be done?
  - What is the benefit of completing this task?
  - Whom does this task benefit?

- This will help the team reflect on whether or not the task matters and how and whom it affects. This will help the team learn to spend time on tasks that add value to the team.

The Kanban system helps every employee add value to his or her task. The goal of the system is that every person performs at least one task that adds to the value of the team. This is a high bar to set for every member of the team. In most companies, Kanban systems are used as agile systems. The teams put their workflow on a board and look at how different tasks will progress over the course of the day or week.

They also visualize certain obstacles and identify ways to overcome those obstacles. However, these systems do not clear the backlog or overload on any team member's desk. It also does not look at how a particular task is adding value to the team.

Most managers prefer agile Kanban systems since they are able to control the process and also collaborate with some members of the team, but they miss the point of the Kanban system. They forget that

- Following the real demand of customers
- Lower any backlog on hand
- Accelerate production flow

Kanban systems cannot function without lean management. A team may be improving continuously over the years, however, if there are no tools available to assess the value added to the team, the improvements made cannot be lean.

A Kanban system must assess how the value of a product has increased and how it has helped a team member effectively complete work with few backlogs.

Most organizations have been applying lean tools for years without trying to understand the purpose of those tools. The current tendency is to play with the principles of the Kanban systems and learn the tools.

The latter is demanding since every team must have clarity on what they are trying to learn and also identify a way to apply what has been learned.

# Chapter Nine: How can Kanban help in Forecasting

It is surprising how organizations still apply practices of shamans and clairvoyants to predict the future. They believe that they use big data to understand the behavior of the customers and the market.

But, the truth is that the organizations trust their development teams to give them the right estimates. Instead of that, an organization can use Kanban boards to obtain estimates based on actual data and statistics.

## Myth of Estimates

It is important to remember that predictability does not increase when one makes a prediction. The capability of any system is not affected by an estimate made on how long it will take for a team to complete a task. It is important to remember that predictability is a property of the system. If an organization fails to realize that, it will never be able to predict the behavior of the system.

## Science behind prediction

It is easy to estimate the time an individual may take to complete a task since there is some data to back the estimate. It is a very different thing to estimate the time it will take a system to move a task from the initial point to the delivery point.

If someone asks, "When do you think it will be done by?" they mean to ask you "When do you think the product will be in the production state?"

No member in the organization has a clue and they often guess or lie about the time. There are instances when an organization has both lied and guessed. It is dangerous to make an estimate, and sometimes a waste of time since the estimate is being calculated using the wrong data. The organization must take time to investigate data before making a claim. However, they do not have the time or the resources to do so.

### Information Theory

When the organization makes an estimate, there is limited data available. It is best to make an estimate at a later stage when there is more data available as the project moves on. It is for this reason that it is recommended that a business use incremental and iterative development and funding.

### Mathematics

If two variables are linearly dependent on each other, any fluctuations that arise in other variables is dependent on the maximum deviation that is calculated by the preceding variables.

### Queuing Theory

The lead-time always increases when resources are highly utilized in systems with variation.

### Lean

Flow efficiency is typically low for most organizations, which means that the lead-time is often influenced by environmental factors.

Therefore, lead-time is not sensitive to the complexity or size of a single feature in the project or specific to the people or their skillset.

# Product Development Approaches

## *Traditional Project Management*

Traditional project management uses the following constraints to make an estimate":

- Schedule
- Scope
- Budget

A budget is set aside and the schedule and scope are agreed upon once the organization has planned and obtained an estimate.

## *Agile*

Agile does not make the commitments made by traditional project management. There is a delivery date agreed upon by the organization, but the scope of the project is flexible. The scope can be defined in a broad sense, but the finer details evolve over time.

## *Kanban*

The Kanban software does not make a promise or commit to a delivery date based on uncertain factors. If Kanban systems are implemented, the organization will agree that there will be a regular delivery of high-quality products. Kanban offers a commitment to each class of service and gives the organization the opportunity to commit to regular delivery, transparency, continuous improvement of quality and lead-time.

# How can this be done?

## *Develop your Kanban system*

The first step would be to design a proper and structured Kanban system. You must understand the demand, delivery, boundaries of the system, different categories of work, policies, classes of service and other attributes. If an organization wants to create a predictable system, it must identify the start and final point of a process. It is within these boundaries where you can make your estimates.

## *Adopt the principles and practices*

The organization must adopt the four principles and six practices of the Kanban tool. These allow the delivery systems to become predictable over time.

## *Understand Variability*

Predictability can be improved using Kanban tools by reducing any variability within the system. Lead Time Histograms, Lead Time Scatterplots and Cumulative Flow Diagrams are the best way to understand how the system is performing and detect the areas that need to be improved.

Variability is considered to be a necessary evil and is required if an organization wishes to innovate processes but not to the point that the process is fully unpredictable.

It is important to allow for some level of variability in the initial stages of the process but not in the development stage of the process. An organization can never have frequent bugs in production, unreliable processes, too many dependencies with other teams and queues in every team to manage the processes and tasks being taken care of by members of the team.

Some sources of variability are:

- Internal:
    - Irregular Flow
    - Work Item Size
    - Class-of-Service Mix
    - Work Item Type Mix
    - Rework
- External:
    - Requirements Ambiguity
    - Irregular Flow
    - Batch Size
    - Environment Availability
    - Expedite Requests
    - Difficulty Scheduling Coordination Activities
    - Other Market Factors
    - Humans

# Forecasting

Depending on how an organization uses Kanban, it will be able to forecast some work items three to four weeks after implementing Kanban. If the implementation is effective, the organization can also forecast some full projects. Let us take a look at how this can be done.

## *Forecasting of Single Features*

Most companies tend to push processes into development lines under the assumption that these processes will be done eventually. They do not understand the capability of the members in the development team. These companies forget that the system becomes slower when the pipeline is clogged with many development tasks leading to undue stress and many errors.

Unless some data is collected using a predictable system, the organization cannot end this vicious cycle. Customers and stakeholders will continue to ask for estimates when they realize that the organization has stopped delivering on time.

Development teams will continue to lie and the tasks are pushed between departments in the hope that at least something will eventually get done. This creates a slower and unpredictable system which makes the business or operations team push more work into the pipeline.

When an organization uses Kanban for at least three weeks, it will have enough data to map to a lead-time histogram. This will help the organization provide an accurate prediction or forecast. The 85th percentile is often used to make a scheduling decision. If the organization starts too early with forecasting, it will sacrifice the opportunity to do something better with the resources it has available.

If it is done too late, there is a risk of incurring a cost of delay. As an organization, the following questions must be asked before beginning making predictions:

- When can this task begin?
- Should this task be put on hold so we can work on other tasks?
- Has it become too late for us to start with this task?
- What is the risk of delaying this task?
- Should other options be sacrificed if the risk is too little?
- If the risk is high, should other tasks be ignored?
- How much will it cost the company if we delay the product?
- How will the customers react?

## *Forecasting of Multiple Features*

Troy Magennis, in his website www.focusedobjective.com, has developed many tools that will help an organization monitor and predict the development of software and other products. His website contains many resources that can be used for free.

You can forecast multiple features using Monte Carlo Simulations and also calculate the probabilities associated with each forecast based on historical data.

# Conclusion

The Kanban system was built by Taiichi Ohno for Toyota automotive in the early 1940s. The method was later defined and used by David Anderson in 2004 in an IT company after which many companies from different industries began to use the tool to improve their functions.

Through Kanban systems, an organization can identify the different processes that must be completed to achieve the final goal. The board lists out these processes and segregates them into the different stages they are in. This also allows the team or the members to identify potential bottlenecks and also find ways to resolve them.

Over the course of the book, you will gather information on how Kanban can be used by different departments to improve quality and also deliver products on time. Kanban systems can also be used to derive estimates for delivery of products through some statistical tools.

To conclude, the Kanban system is an effective tool, which helps to maintain transparency, thereby giving the organization an understanding of how work is progressing between different departments.

Thank you for purchasing the book. I hope you have gathered the information you were looking for.

# Resources

https://www.digite.com/kanban/what-is-kanban/

https://www.smartsheet.com/understanding-kanban-inventory-management-and-its-uses-across-multiple-industries

https://www.leonardogroupamericas.com/go/index.php/manufacturing-blog/94-is-kanban-obsolete

https://www.digite.com/blog/has-kanban-truly-arrived-for-project-management/

https://gerardchiva.com/2017/01/21/predictability-in-kanban-systems/

http://www.djaa.com/project-management-kanban-part-3-forecasting

https://news.ibqmi.org/six-types-of-kanban-explained

https://www.leankor.com/what-departments-can-use-kanban-boards/

https://www.lean.org/balle/DisplayObject.cfm?o=3298

https://leankanban.com/kanbans-change-management-principles/

https://blog.crisp.se/2013/10/21/mattiasskarin/enterprise-kanban-improving-the-full-value-chain-using-lean-thinking

https://dzone.com/articles/working-with-kanban-frequently-asked-questions

www.ingramcontent.com/pod-product-compliance
Lightning Source LLC
Chambersburg PA
CBHW071237220526
45468CB00002B/890